MAT MCCONAUGHEY

From Limelight to Greenlight,

The Multifaceted World of

Matthew Mcconaughey

LIZA MICHAEL

CONTENTS

CHAPTER THREE

INSIDE MATTHEW MCCONAUGHEY

RELATIONSHIP LIFE
   Ashely Judd
   Sandra Bullock
   Penelope Cruz
   Camila Alves

REFLECTIONS ON FAME, FAMILY, AND FORMATIVE YEAR
   Love and Loss
   The Cataclysm in Texas: McConaughey's Unyielding
   Devotion
   Dealing With Career Ups and Downs
   Dealing with His father's death
   Missing opportunities to work on the Titanic
   Avoiding Typecast
   Self-Criticism and Constant Search for perfection
   Tested by Fame: The Mother-Son Bond
   Working to Survive
   Dealing with physical and verbal abuse
   The Strange Life Overseas
   A Glimpse into the Complex Dynamics of Family Love

SOCIAL LIFE AND MORE
   A Lover of Animals
   MJM
   Giving Back to the University Community
   The Just Keep Livin' Foundation

CHAPTER FOUR

A CHRONOLOGY OF MCCONAUGHEY'S CONTROVERSIES

CHAPTER FIVE

CONCLUSION

PREAMBLE

In the glittering world of Hollywood, here is a man whose name could be heard in the lights and sounds of the city. Who is he? Matthew McConaughey.

"Dazed and Confused," a comedy that got better with age like a good wine, was the first movie that made him a star. Word got around that he was one of the best who had ever been on the big screen. Before he became famous, his figure appeared in TV commercials, and he played minor parts in movies that were just starting out. Then, like a storm that throws a person into a wild relationship, fate brought him to a movie called "A Time to Kill," which he worked on with the master Joel Schumacher. The big screen took him in with all its glory, and soon parts started coming at him like leaves in the fall. From there, he went on to play a wide range of parts that put his name in the history books of Hollywood.

Imagine this charming Texan who didn't want to do what his family did. He was born into a middle-class family with business connections, but he was different from his brothers in that he was brave enough to dance to a different beat. McConaughey was a free spirit who chose his own path. Through a student exchange program, he had the chance to go to Australia, a part that would change his story in ways he could not have imagined.

The bright rays of the new millennium shone on Matthew McConaughey's face, and a new phase began. But the sands of time can shape even the hardest rocks into different shapes. In 2011, McConaughey's life took a turn that led him down a road less traveled: acting in serious, emotional parts. The world saw how talented he was in movies such as "Magic Mike," "The Lincoln Lawyer," and "Bernie."

The story of McConaughey goes beyond what the camera could show. He has also used his fame as a sign of hope by starting the "Just Keep Livin Foundation" to help high school students live better, more independent lives.

As his journey goes on, his parts get better, like wine gets better with age. Time magazine named him one of the "Most Influential People in the World," a tribute to the waves he made and the stories he told.

So, Matthew McConaughey's journey is a symphony of parts, interests, and goals that spanned decades and fields. In the middle of Hollywood's sky, he wasn't just a star—he was a constellation, with each point telling a story and each light showing the way for those who came after him.

This will be an interesting trip through the pages of McConaughey's life, where the threads of fate made a story of love, strength, and change.

But let's not be fooled by the bright lights of fame. Every star has its own story, a road that has been shaped by the trials of life. Behind the sets of the movies, Matthew McConaughey's life story is also written with ink that bled from the wounds of a hard youth. His early years were like a fabric made of strands of strength and the shadows of terrible events. Yet, like a phoenix rising from the ashes, he faced the storms and came out of them stronger, showing that he had an unbreakable spirit.

Life, like a great writer, sets up its scenes in surprising ways. Fame came to him later in life, making dreams that seemed as far away as the stars come true. But when the curtain went up on his fame, it brought with it new problems and unknown territory that only a seasoned man could handle. However, each step, each milestone, was a dance with the unknown, a cascade of experiences that shaped him into the gem he would become.

As we go through this story, we learn that every star and soul in the world is made by the hands of time and the creator of experiences. Matthew McConaughey's life, which is both bright and dark, is an example. It is a painting that shows how the human spirit can survive, change, and shine light into even the darker parts of life.

So, the story goes on, a story filled with the colors of love, strength, and change. A story that speaks to us from the pages of

McConaughey's life, telling us that each of us has the power to make our own star, something that will shine in the sky long after we've taken our last bow.

CHAPTER ONE

THE EARLY YEARS OF MATTHEW MCCONAUGHEY'S LIFE

BIRTH

On November 4, 1969, a star was born in a small Texas town called Uvalde. Matthew David McConaughey was born to a man named James Donald McConaughey, who ran a gas station and sold oil, and a woman named Mary Kathleen, who taught kindergarten and helped shape young minds.

But school brought him back. Matthew studied his interest at the University of Texas, in the Austin College of

Communication, with the city of Austin as a background. Those years weren't just about books and classes; they were also about building relationships and ties that would last a lifetime. This was clear from the fact that he was an involved member of the "Delta Tau Delta International Fraternity." In 1993, when the sun was shining brightly, Matthew held up his Bachelor of Science degree in radio-television-film with pride. It was a sign of how hard he had worked and how many exciting things were still to come.

EDUCATION

Matthew's journey through school began in Uvalde, Texas, which was more than just a place. This town's unique Texas charm would have shaped his early ideas about the world. Here, in a close-knit society, he would have picked up ideals that may have helped him be more stable as an adult.

The McConaughey family chose to accept change as time went on. They moved to Longview, Texas, where they now live. In the hallways and halls of Longview High School, young Matthew first started to make plans for his future.

Longview High School

When McConaughey went to Longview High School, it was a big change in his life. During high school, many of us make friends we'll keep for life, decide on our first job goals, and grow a lot as people. Matthew wasn't just another student. He stood out and made an impact, which is how he got the title "Most Handsome." Aside from his title, it seems likely that he was an involved and energetic student who took part in many school events and laid the groundwork for his future.

Rotary Youth Exchange Program

Matthew's spirit wanted more than just experiences close to home. In 1988, he set out on a long trip to Warnervale, New South Wales, Australia, with a strong desire to see the world. Matthew was happy to be a part of the Rotary Youth Exchange program. For a year, he lived in Australia and learned about its culture, making connections between his home country and the land down there.

This wasn't just a trip abroad for McConaughey; it was a deep dive into another culture. In Warnervale, New South Wales, he would have seen things from a very different point of view than in Texas. Living in Australia for a year, he would have learned about the country's native cultures, tried its unique food, picked up the local slang, and understood how people there live. Such events, especially during a person's developmental years, can have a profound effect on a person, teaching them understanding, adaptability, and a wider view of the world.

University of Texas

McConaughey went to college in the busy city of Austin, which is known for its music, art, and cultural diversity. He would have learned about a wide range of media-related topics at the Austin College of Communication. His education would have covered a wide range of topics, from figuring out how radio waves work to figuring out how movies are made. Since he was surrounded by students, teachers, and industry pros who shared his interests, his love for fun would have grown every day.

Bachelor of Science Degree

Getting his Bachelor of Science in radio-television-film wasn't just a great academic achievement. The world of media is very big, and through his classes, he would have learned a lot about its many different parts. This would have helped him prepare for future jobs in front of and behind the camera.

Delta Tau Delta International Fraternity

College life isn't just about schoolwork; it's also about growing as a person and being part of a group. Since McConaughey was a member of the "Delta Tau Delta International Fraternity," he wasn't just studying. He would have done volunteer work, taken on leadership roles, and gotten to know people in his group. This shows that the student has a healthy college life, with both academic, social, and charitable activities.

Each of these steps in McConaughey's schooling wasn't just a phase or a line on his resume; they were building blocks that helped him become the complex person he is today.

From The Classroom & Beyond

The above is just a summary of Matthew McConaughey's educational journey. However, it's important to remember that he also learned and grew a lot outside of these official settings, such as in Hollywood and other personal projects.

Each of these steps in McConaughey's schooling wasn't just a phase or a line on his resume; they were building blocks that helped him become the complex person he is today. All of Matthew McConaughey's school experiences helped make him the man he is today. He is a mix of his Texas roots, his experiences around the world, his intellectual knowledge, and his strong sense of community.

CHAPTER TWO

CAREER IN ACTING

The 90s

In 1991, Matthew McConaughey was among the newest person to join the exciting world of entertainment. His career didn't start on the big screen though, but in TV commercials, where his charisma first won people over.

Soon after, he was in the movie "**Dazed and Confused**," which became a classic coming-of-age story. The movie got a lot of praise from critics, and it led to a number of different roles. From the haunting echoes of "**Texas Chainsaw Massacre**:

The Next Generation" to the ethereal

"**Angels in the Outfield**" and the touching

moments in "**Boys on the**

Side," McConaughey brought his unique

charm to each.

Five years later, 1996 was a very important

year. In "**A Time to Kill**," directed by Joel

Schumacher, McConaughey went deep

into Jake Brigance's mind. In the movie

version of John Grisham's gripping book,

he gave a performance that won him a lot

of praise, including the MTV Movie Award

for Best Breakthrough Performance.

The next year, 1997, McConaughey went back in time and played a character in the Oscar-nominated historical epic "**Amistad**," which was directed by the great Steven Spielberg, and saw glowing reviews from critics. As the end of the millennium got closer, he embraced Edward "Ed" Pekurny's oddities in Ron Howard's "EDtv" and dove into wartime suspense in "U-571.

2000 - 2009

In a memorable episode of "**Sex and the City**" at the start of the 21st century, he charmed people in the glitzy streets of New

York. In 2001, he showed how romantic he was by putting together love stories in **"The Wedding Planner**." From fighting dragons in **'Reign of Fire'** to figuring out the complicated plots of **'Thirteen Conversations About One Thing**' and **'Frailty'** in 2002, adventure and intrigue were not far behind.

In 2003, his career got even more interesting. In "**Freedom**: A History of Us," he wrote about the story of humanity.

2005 made a colorful picture. In "**Two for the Money,**" McConaughey went deep into the world of sports betting. In "Sahara," he went on an adventure in the desert. In "**Magnificent Desolation**: Walking on the Moon 3D," he gave Al Bean's voice.

So, as the years went by, McConaughey's early film career became a demonstration of his versatility, passion, and unwavering commitment.

In 2006, the world of movies got a story set in history that was both exciting and thought-provoking. Under McG's masterful direction, "**We Are Marshall**" showed the strong spirit of Jack Lengyel, which Matthew McConaughey brought to life.

In 2008, McConaughey was ready to blow people away again with 'Fool's Gold,' which was full of fast-paced adventures. In the hit comedy "**Tropic Thunder**," which came out that same year, he showed how good he was at making people laugh. But there was more to it than just action and jokes. In **'Surfer, Dude**,' as Steve Addington, we saw him ride the waves, which was a great way to show how laid-back surf culture is.

The year 2009 came in with a touch of love and memories. In **'Ghosts of Girlfriends Past**,' McConaughey danced a sad tango with Jennifer Garner. Even though the movie did well at the box office, the critics didn't applaud.

2010 & Beyond

In 2010, the comedy show "**Eastbound & Down**" on the famous HBO network showed off his acting skills. He left an indelible mark through three events that people will never forget. As the year went on, he moved into the world of law and became the main character in 'The Lincoln Lawyer.'

Later, in the powerful movie "**Mud**," he dealt with the problems of growing up, while "**Magic Mike**" and "**The Paperboy**" added to his filmography.

On the other hand, the awards started coming in, with the New York Film Critics Circle Award as the crown jewel for his great work in "**Bernie**" and "**Magic Mike**." He also won the National Society of Film Critics Award and the prestigious Independent Spirit Award for "**Magic Mike**."

Then came 2013, which was a golden year. "**Dallas Buyers Club**" wasn't just a movie; it showed how McConaughey can change into different characters. He played a cowboy with AIDS, and his performance was so real and moving that people all over the world stood up and took notice. But beyond the statues, this part of McConaughey's life was full of recognition, respect, and a legacy that keeps growing. He won both the Academy Award and the Golden Globe for Best Actor, which are the highest awards in the movie business.

In the busy middle of 2013, movie fans flocked to see **'The Wolf of Wall Street**,' which was a very interesting story. Matthew McConaughey, who was part of a great cast, had a moment in the spotlight that held people's attention.

HBO showed off its new crime series, **"True Detective**." From the very first episode, viewers were treated to McConaughey's masterful transformation into Rust Cohle, a brooding detective who navigated the dark alleys of crime. This performance wasn't just strong; it was transcendent. It won him a lot of awards, including a nomination for a Primetime Emmy and praise from the Golden Globes. In the end, the Critics' Choice Television Award named him the Best Actor of that year, and the Golden Globes were looking at him again in 2015.

As 2014 began, the movie "**Interstellar**" showed how space and time are connected. McConaughey played NASA pilot Joseph Cooper, and he took the audience on a journey through space that was both sad and beautiful. The talented Michael Caine, Matt Damon, Jessica Chastain, and Anne Hathaway were all in the movie, which was directed by Christopher Nolan, who had a lot of ideas. What about prizes? "Interstellar" won the Oscar for Best Visual Effects, and it was also nominated for a lot of other awards.

McConaughey's journey went on and on, just as he tried new things. He also gave voice to animated characters in "**Kubo and the Two Strings**" and "**Sing**," and he played different characters in movies like "**The Sea of Trees**" and "**The Dark Tower**."

McConaughey's name was talked about a lot at award shows. He was nominated for Best Actor at the 2015 Academy of Science Fiction, Fantasy, and Horror Films, USA Awards, and he won a Saturn Award for "**Killer Joe**" in 2013.

But was that all? The day movies gave him a place in history. On November 17, 2014, a cool Monday, Matthew McConaughey's star sparkled on the Hollywood Walk of Fame. As the golden statuette of the Oscar for "Dallas Buyers Club" shone in his cabinet, McConaughey invited the world to a celebration, not of fame, but of art and family. Today, he will always be remembered as a great actor in the history of movies.

SATURDAY NIGHT LIVE

First Time Out

Matthew McConaughey's first time on "Saturday Night Live" (SNL) was a shining example of how much of a star he is. This dynamic appearance by a famous actor in the late 1990s wasn't just another celebrity cameo. It showed a star coming out of the shadows of his well-known film roles and ready to take on comedy with the same passion as his dramatic roles. Matthew's comedic skills were shown in a new and fun way, which set the stage for future work together.

Putting on SNL

In 2015, when McConaughey hosted SNL, it was clear that he wasn't just there to promote a movie or project. He was there to impress people. In his opening monologue, he talked about the history of his famous "Alright, alright, alright" catchphrase in a way that was both funny and brought back memories.

McConaughey's energy as a host made it clear that he was just as comfortable on a live comedy stage as he was on a movie set.

Notable Sketches

Each sketch McConaughey was in became its own mini-event. In a touching and funny Thanksgiving skit, he played a father who had grown apart from his family. This gave the comedy more depth. In a riskier, more unusual skit, he played a person who was taken by aliens. This lets his quirky side shine. These sketches were a great example of how versatile

McConaughey was. They showed that he could play any character, no matter how strange, and make it his own.

SNL Legacy

In a nutshell, Matthew McConaughey's interactions with "Saturday Night Live" have been more than just appearances. They have been big cultural moments that show how deep and varied an actor can be when he doesn't let expectations limit him. McConaughey's magic doesn't change whether he's playing a serious role or making people laugh on Saturday Night Live.

McConaughey's appearances on SNL gave him more than just laughs and applause. They also helped him build a legacy that very few actors can claim. He was a complete performer, not just a dramatic hero or a romantic lead. Since then, his SNL sketches have become part of popular culture, making him not only a movie icon but also a master of comedy. His move into comedy, especially with SNL, also showed that he didn't want to be put into just one category.

CHAPTER THREE

INSIDE MATTHEW MCCONAUGHEY

RELATIONSHIP LIFE

Ashely Judd

Matthew McConaughey was first drawn to the beautiful Ashley Judd in the neon-lit world of movies, where people's lives often cross paths in strange ways. The first time they met on the big screen was in the 1996 thriller "A Time to Kill." In this scene, Ashley played Carla, the wife of Jake Tyler Brigance, who was played by Matthew McConaughey. Their on-screen chemistry was palpable, and it lit up the screens with hints of an off-screen romance in the making.

But, like a movie plot twist, McConaughey's feelings soon turned in a different direction. It was said that he liked another co-star from the same movie. His relationship with Ashley came to an end slowly.

But in 1996 and 1997, the strong Ashley, who was known for her poise, seemed to find comfort in the arms of the soulful singer Michael Bolton. Even though it was short, their beautiful duet showed how

Ashley's love journey was always changing.

In the next part of her story, engines roared and she felt the thrill of going fast. She couldn't get enough of the handsome race car driver Dario Franchitti. Their love story, which began in 2001 and lasted until 2013, was another thrilling race of love and friendship.

In the big picture of Hollywood, where relationships come and go as quickly as movie roles, McConaughey and Ashley both found love, lost it, and found it again on their own paths.

Sandra Bullock

McConaughey lived in Hollywood, where the stories are as lively as the stars in the sky. He was eager and wild, so he didn't think twice about falling in love under the bright studio lights. Even though his relationship with Ashley didn't last long, fate had other plans.

In 1996, on the set of "A Time to Kill," where cameras were clicking and lines were being rehearsed, his heartbeat with Sandra Bullock's. By that time, Sandra had already made a name for herself in movie history. Her roles in "Speed" and "While You Were Sleeping" had wowed audiences all over the world. The times they spent together were sweet, but as the reels of time turned, after two passionate years, they decided to stop seeing each other, but not in a harsh way.

In 2003, when Sandra was almost 56 and had grown up, she talked about the whispers from the past. She told the world with real warmth how their relationship had changed but never broken. They stayed friends for a long time because they respected and cared deeply for each other. She told everyone that getting married or having other ties would not break this bond.

Both of them found comfort in the small-town charm of Austin, Texas. While McConaughey and his girlfriend Camila made a home there, Sandra was also drawn to its beauty. She fell in love with it for the first time when she was filming "Hope Floats" in 1998. As the years went by, Sandra found another muse in the camera of Bryan Randall in 2015. However, her friendship with McConaughey didn't change, which shows that some stories are timeless.

Penelope Cruz

In another story of love, Matthew McConaughey couldn't stay away from the beautiful Penélope Cruz, who was in his most recent movie. With her sparkling eyes and the spirit of 46 summers, she quickly became the main character in his story which didn't happen on screen.

More than just scripts and spotlights brought them together. As soon as the clapperboard said "cut," the two went on an exciting road trip through the colorful landscapes of Mexico. Even though there wasn't much room in McConaughey's camper, they got closer and found out how well they fit together.

Yet, as in many Hollywood stories, their lives took different turns in 2006. Hollywood's fast-paced lifestyle ended their relationship, but as one chapter ended, another one began. In the middle of a busy West Hollywood club that same year, McConaughey and Camila's eyes met. The spell worked right away.

As time went on, Javier Bardem, a Spanish master who had won an Oscar, came into Penélope's life in 2010. The two began their own love story because they shared a passion and a job.

Camila Alves

From where he was, he tried to catch her eye so he could call her over quietly. But when they briefly looked at each other, Matthew knew right away that she wasn't just any woman who could be called from far away. No, Camila was not just anyone. He got up from his seat and pushed his way through the crowd to get to her.

His eyes, which were usually calm and collected, widened in surprise when he realized what he had just said. He didn't wonder what her name was when he saw her. Instead, he asked, "What is this enchanting presence?"

After just three nights, they went on their first date under a blanket of stars. And from that moment on, Matthew knew he would never need to spend another romantic evening with anyone else. Time went by quickly, and in 2008, Levi, who is now 15 years old and full of life, brought them a bundle of joy. And the family's story kept getting better. In the years after that, they had Vida, a bright-eyed girl who is now twelve, and then Livingston, a lively boy who is now nine.

Their hearts beat in perfect time, and it didn't take long before Matthew and Camila decided to make their love official. On June 9, 2012, a day to remember, they said their vows. Their journey, which began when they met by chance in 2006, is still another great example of how magical love can be.

REFLECTIONS ON FAME, FAMILY, AND FORMATIVE YEAR

Love and Loss

In the big picture of life, there is a connection that speaks deeply to the human spirit and gets to the heart of what it means to be alive. This connection is often shown by a wagging tail, a wet nose, and four paws. Dogs, these amazing creatures who love and care for each other no matter what, don't just have the ability to be pets; they can also mirror our deepest feelings and wants. Their loyalty and love for everyone are so strong that they often leave permanent marks on our hearts that can never be erased. They don't just become extra parts of our stories; they become the main parts.

Even the famous actor Matthew McConaughey found comfort and company in his furry friend in the world of stars and the spotlight. He once told Oprah Winfrey a sad story about his beloved half-labrador, half-chow dog, Ms. Hud.

This story isn't about glitz and glamour. Instead, it's about heart, soul, and how time moves on no matter what. Her journey began in a small place in Tucson, Arizona, in a pound. But fate had other plans, and McConaughey let her into his life because he was charmed by her spirit. Over the course of 12 years, they traveled all across

America, discovering its vastness and making many memories along the way.

But like all stories, theirs had a dark side. Cancer once hurt Ms. Hud so badly that she had to have one of her front legs cut off. But she didn't give up. Her spirit was strong. But life had another junction. After falling out of bed one night, McConaughey had to face the harsh reality that her back legs were paralyzed. As soon as the sun came up, a trip to the vet made it clear that the choice that lay ahead was a sad one.

With a heavy heart, he took a moment to think about how good his best friend's life might be. It wasn't just about the present, but also about the pain and trouble she might face in the future. And in that teary moment, with love, respect, and a great deal of sadness, McConaughey made the hardest choice of all: to let Ms. Hud go.

The Cataclysm in Texas: McConaughey's Unyielding Devotion

Matthew McConaughey was born and raised under the big Texas sky, and he is proud of his roots. Texas isn't just a state to him; it's a rich blend of memories, values, and culture that runs through his veins. During his conversation on "Popcorn with Peter Travers," McConaughey's eyes lit up like a fire, a fire that was fueled by his deep love and pride for his home country. His beautiful words painted a clear picture of the spirit of Texas and the strong heartbeat of its people, which he feels so deeply.

So, when a tragedy happened in June 2022 in the middle of his hometown, Uvalde, McConaughey didn't just watch. He became a source of strength and support for his community. As CNN and other news outlets reported, McConaughey and his caring wife Camilla reached out to the grieving families and stood side by side with those whose lives had been violently upended by this tragedy. They didn't just go to these homes because they were famous. They went because they cared about the people there and because they had felt the same pain.

But McConaughey's commitment was more than just words and actions. He used the fact that he was a famous person to take his passionate plea to the White House, where decisions are made. He fought hard for stricter gun control laws and asked everyone to come together, stressing how important it was to work together for the good of all Americans. Every time he spoke, he talked about his dream of a united country where people care about each other and work to improve the lives of everyone.

Dealing With Career Ups and Downs

In the glittering world of movies, where success is often measured by how well a movie does at the box office and how many awards it wins, he stood out, not just because of the awards he won but also because of the unique path he took. Even though he has won many awards over the years, including the prestigious Academy Award, he is honest about the fact that he has not had consistent commercial success. He has been in a lot of interesting movies, but not all of them have done well at the box office. But this part of his memoir, "Greenlights," is not a sad story; it is a story of passion. Every movie and role he plays is an act of love for him. Even when his movies don't do well at the box office, he doesn't let it get him down. If anything, it makes him even more dedicated to his work.

At this point in his career, he is more than just a performer. He is an actor and an artist who looks for and finds satisfaction in the depth and variety of his roles. But in 2017, The Guardian looked at what seemed to be a dip in his film career and suggested that another break might give him a new start, a "McConaissance," if you will. The year before had been especially hard, with movies like "Free State of Jones" not doing well and "The Sea of Trees" getting a lot of bad reviews at Cannes. But every artist goes through ups and downs, and he continues to amaze, inspire, and grow thanks to his strong spirit and hard work.

Though it had a lot of potential, the movie didn't do well at the box office, which was a sad thing in the world of movies, which is full of passion, dreams, and reality. Even though the actor had put everything he had into the role, the cruel turn of events made him lose interest. Not only did it hurt him emotionally, but it also changed his body in a noticeable way. He put on more weight for the role, and getting back to his old shape was going to be a Herculean task. In fact, in 2019, Matthew McConaughey talked openly about his journey to get fit again, with every drop of sweat being a sign of his determination.

But that wasn't the only change he went through to play the part. The long hair was gone, and in its place was a shaved head, which was a clear sign of his commitment. Even though he made so many sacrifices, the critics weren't impressed, and he didn't get any praise.

Ironically, McConaughey's earlier work in "Dallas Buyers Club" showed a different kind of physical sacrifice. He lost almost 50 pounds and looked like a skeleton when he came back out. This change made a big impression on people and showed them how dedicated he was. Such is the unpredictable pattern of an actor's life, which is made up of victories, setbacks, and unwavering commitment.

Dealing with His father's death

There are times in life that change the way the threads of our lives are woven together forever. In 1992, Matthew McConaughey's heart was broken when he lost his father, James Donald McConaughey. It left him with a deep hole in his heart.

On a calm evening, McConaughey opened up to Tim Ferriss about how much this loss changed the direction of his life. Grief, in its strange way, had opened a door inside of him. The fact that life is short has become more clear than ever. The bright lights of the stage, the sound of the applause, and the allure of being a star were things he had always wanted, but now they seemed like they would not last. This realization, with its sad beauty, gave him strength. Fear kept him from taking the known paths, so he embraced the unknown and went into uncharted areas of his career. He was willing to embrace change and take risks.

But the story of his family had more to tell, stories of love that was passionate and hard. His parents' love story was the stuff of legend. Their love was like a whirlwind because they got married, broke up, got back together, and then broke up again. But they always came back to each other, like two stars locked in a dance that would never end. And in a twist of fate that was as beautiful as their love story, James died when he was close to the person he loved. When his mother told him this news, it was so heavy that McConaughey's knees buckled and his world went fuzzy as he couldn't believe what he was hearing. It showed how much love, loss, and life lessons had changed him.

Missing opportunities to work on the Titanic

With his magnetic charm and undeniable talent, Matthew McConaughey moved with grace through the bright world of movies, where dreams often become real. But sometimes, even the brightest stars miss the constellations they are trying to reach. And so did McConaughey, whose journey included some roads he didn't take.

Imagine this... Everyone knows and loves Leonardo DiCaprio as the free-spirited Jack, McConaughey's name used to be heard in those casting rooms. In fact, the ethereal Kate Winslet once told a story about an audition scene where she and McConaughey were both in it. What a great match they could have made!

But McConaughey missed more than just the Titanic opportunity. The Hulk, who was strong and angry, was another character. He had always liked the idea of being the green giant in Marvel. But, unfortunately, when he knocked on Marvel's big doors and said he wanted to be the Hulk, he was politely turned away. The reasons stayed hidden in the quiet hallways of the movie business. Even though Edward Norton wore the green of the Hulk in "The Incredible Hulk" in 2008, Mark Ruffalo became the face of the beastly hero in the Marvel Cinematic Universe as a whole.

Even though McConaughey moved on, one can only wonder and hope about the magic he could make if given the chance.

Avoiding Typecast

In the golden age of Hollywood, the early 2000s told a story that many people were interested in. During these years, Matthew McConaughey, who was the star of many people's hearts, chose to step back into the background and go on a journey that became known as the "McConaissance."

With his charming smile and heartwarming stories, the silver screen's "lover-boy" was starting to feel like he was stuck in a world where everything was romantic comedies. The scripts that landed on his desk started to run together and sound like the same tunes. Matthew's heart longed for different beats and scripts that would push him and make him dance to different beats.

He did something brave that was both brave and inspiring. At a crossroads where he had to make a choice, he saw an offer for $14.5 million. It was another romantic story. But he knew what he was worth and what his dreams were. He turned down the allure of such a well-paying job and went deeper into his sabbatical to try to start over.

During these months of silence, when everyone was waiting for him to come back, McConaughey changed. He compared this time of change to coming up with a "new idea," which is a beautiful way of saying "finding again." And as time went on, the choice he made paid off. The horizon grew, and roles that were more different from each other began to call to him.

Self-Criticism and Constant Search for perfection

Matthew McConaughey's life has been a mix of shining successes and quiet times. He was born and raised in Hollywood, where new stars are born every day. In 2018, a story in The Guardian showed a side of the actor that is rarely seen: he is an artist who is always trying to reach a dream that is just beyond his reality.

Matthew has done a lot of great things, but he can't seem to be satisfied. Every script and every role sparks a dream of what could be. But every time the curtain falls, he feels like the real thing didn't quite live up to the brilliance of his dream.

This kind of self-reflection shows how humble McConaughey is. He is not afraid to think about himself or even criticize himself. Even though he's proud of some of his roles and thinks he did them justice, he hasn't found his "magnum opus," a role or movie that lives up to his highest hopes.

He has a spirit that is always looking for perfection, which may never be reached. But it's his constant drive to be the best, his never-ending pursuit of the perfect dream, that keeps him growing and making sure that his star, which was already bright, keeps getting brighter.

Tested by Fame: The Mother-Son Bond

Matthew McConaughey grew up in the heart of Texas, where stories are as big as the sky. His mother, Kay, cared for him and kept him safe. Their relationship, which proved the old saying, was stronger than any script he would later write. As time went on, Matthew's talent put him on the road to becoming a star. But he had no idea that his fame would put the relationship he valued at risk.

As the flashbulbs lit up his life, Matthew could see that Kay had changed. It seemed like her son's rising star was drawing her in and making her feel high. Those sacred, everyday moments, like their weekly phone calls, started to feel less like catching up with their mothers and more like press briefings. It seemed like his mother had turned into a fan, eagerly watching his life in the spotlight.

"The realization broke my heart". Matthew tried to get through these rough waters by telling his mother what it was like to be famous. But he couldn't believe it when their private conversations made the news. The evening news picked up on their private moments, which caused both of them to feel a pain they hadn't expected.

Because of the weight of betrayal and miscommunication, there was an emotional chasm of eight years of silence. But time, which is the best healer, brought them back together in the end. Their Mother-Son Bond was Tested by

Fame, but it held up. Even though they both had scars, they were able to love and understand each other again.

Working to Survive

In Texas, where dreams often seem bigger than life, Matthew McConaughey, when he was young, found his way through the unpredictable streets of Hollywood. Today, his name is big and bright on marquees, but it wasn't always that way.

Years before the camera loved him, he got a lot of rejection letters, which made him doubt himself while he was in film school. Then, something unexpected happened:

while many people were impressed by his charisma, a talent agent was drawn in by his hands. The agent thought that maybe he could start out as a hand model. But there was a small catch: Matthew had to stop biting his nails when he was nervous and start taking good care of his hands.

But dreams of making it big on the big screen were still far away, and bills were very real. So, to make money, he put on an apron and worked at the Catfish Station. This wasn't just any bar; it was a cultural melting pot full of catfish, beer, and soulful blues music. Matthew's fair skin made him stand out in this world. He was like a single

star in the Texas sky. But it was here,

among the strong smells and blues sounds,

that he became close with the pub owner,

a friendship that has stood the test of time

and fame.

Dealing with physical and verbal abuse

Matthew McConaughey, in the course of

speaking up about his experiences in

Greenlights, has also been upfront about

some of the most painful things he's lived

through in his life. He expressed that his

first experience with sex was unpleasant

and that he was basically coerced into it.

He also said that it was his first time having sexual contact. He stated that he was 15 years old at the time it occurred and that it was a case of blackmail. He wrote that he was certain he was going to hell for the premarital intercourse. On the other hand, at this point in time, all he can say with certainty is that he sincerely hopes that is not the case. He also mentioned that he was abused at a later time, specifically when he was 18 years old, and was assaulted by a man who was significantly older than him. The actor believes that he has never been in a position where he could be considered a victim, despite the fact that he has been through a number of challenging circumstances in his life. He added a bright note following the gloomy information and said that he has a lot of proof that the world is conspiring to make him happy.

The Strange Life Overseas

In his book, "Greenlights," Matthew McConaughey tells an important part of his childhood story in a very real way. As soon as he graduated from high school, he was on a plane to Australia as part of an exchange program. But Australia showed McConaughey a very different picture than the one he had made up in his mind.

He ended up living with a strange family in the Australian outback, which is a large, wild area. He was far from busy cities and beautiful coasts, and all he could see was the vast horizon.

Life as he knew it came to a strange stop. Matthew was very alone. He didn't have any close friends, his job was unstable, and he didn't even have a basic phone, so he couldn't even hear the voices of his loved ones. But in this time alone, he saw an opportunity. A chance to dig deep, rely on his own strength and come up with a plan to be self-reliant.

When he thinks back on that year, McConaughey can see how much of an impact it had on him. The struggles of that Australian odyssey, with all its ups and downs, helped him become the strong superstar he would become. He knows that if that year hadn't been so hard, his life might have gone in a totally different direction after that.

A Glimpse into the Complex Dynamics of Family Love

As a child, he had his share of stormy times, and sometimes the threat of violence loomed over him. But in his heart, he didn't think it was fair to call his parents "abusive." He knew that most people would see his parents' behaviors through the lens of worry, but even though he was afraid, Matthew still felt a strong sense of love in his house. No matter how calm or crazy things were, his parents' love for him and his siblings never changed.

When he became a father, McConaughey gained a new point of view. He knows that the way he raises his children is very different from how he was raised. Even though he remembered getting in trouble in the past and being punished for it, he is careful to create an open setting for communication with his children, which is something he thought was missing from his own childhood. McConaughey gives a deep look at how love, discipline, and understanding work in a family through these discoveries.

SOCIAL LIFE AND MORE

A Lover of Animals

As the crisp winter wind of 2021 rustled through the trees, things were about to get a little livelier and a lot furrier in the McConaughey house. Matthew McConaughey and his beautiful wife, Camila, had not one but two tiny gifts of joy with wagging tails in the middle of January.

The Humane Society's good work helped this couple find a happy home for these two sweet puppies, who both had stories of overcoming obstacles.

The older puppy, a little soul with sparkling eyes, was only 4 months old. Its younger sister, a lively ball of fur, was only 2 months old. The happiness in the house was obvious, and the beautiful Brazilian supermodel Camila caught this happiness in a moving picture with one of their new pet family members.

In spite of all the happiness and dog cuddles, she made a joke about how busy

McConaughey's life was about to get. Between their three wonderful children, the two older dogs who were taking care of them, the excited new puppies, the purring cat, and her beloved mother-in-law, the house was sure to be full of laughter, chaos, and memories.

MJM

Mack, Jack & McConaughey (MJ&M) is a fundraising attempt by singer-songwriter Jack Ingram, ESPN reporter and former Texas head coach Mack Brown, and Academy Award-winning actor Matthew McConaughey. The partnership began in 2013 with the goal of raising money and publicity for nonprofits that help children. Most of the time, the MJ&M event has a dinner, music, a fashion show, and a golf game. The money raised goes to groups that help kids with their schooling, health, and well-being.

Years have passed since the inception of the Mack, Jack & McConaughey Foundation, and it was time to celebrate. The star-studded trio – actor Matthew McConaughey, country music artist Jack Ingram, and the University of North Carolina football coach Mack Brown – the foundation commemorated its ten-year anniversary in grand style.

The celebratory event was nothing short of spectacular. Hosted by McConaughey and his wife, the soiree kicked off with a dazzling fashion show, graced by designs from the renowned Stella McCartney. But the spotlight wasn't merely on high fashion; the sounds of country music echoed throughout the venue, with Kenny Chesney taking the stage to delight attendees with a headlining performance.

However, beyond the glitz, glamour, and entertainment, the foundation's mission remained at the heart of the event. Established with a deep-seated commitment to children's initiatives, the Mack, Jack & McConaughey Foundation has, over the years, made a significant impact. With a focus on enhancing children's health, education, and safety, the foundation's efforts have borne fruit. Their tireless work has translated into a whopping $20 million in donations, funds which have been directed towards a myriad of non-profits striving to uplift young lives.

A decade in, and the foundation's legacy of giving continues to shine brightly, illuminating the path for many more years

of philanthropy and positive change.

Giving Back to the University Community

In the busy city of Austin, Texas, in the

heart of Texas, where the University of

Texas is, Matthew McConaughey took on a

part that wasn't for the movies. His well-

known face wasn't just in movie ads; his

laughter and knowledge could be heard in

the halls of the Department of Radio-

Television-Film. By 2019, people on

campus were talking about how

McConaughey was no longer just a

graduate, but also a professor of practice.

It wasn't his first time in the classroom, though. Since 2015, he has been teaching as a visiting professor there.

But McConaughey's dedication to the school he went to didn't stop with classes and talks. In 2016, as the night in Texas got darker and the stars got brighter, many students needed a safe way to get home. The student council came up with the great idea of SURE Walk, which lets people walk together or take a golf cart ride at night. Who, you might ask, was seen driving one of these golf carts at one time? The individual responsible for the action in question was McConaughey

himself. The moment was so touching

that the happy students couldn't help but

post a picture of their ride under the stars

online for everyone to see.

The Just Keep Livin' Foundation

Camila and Matthew McConaughey

started to dream under the warm Texas

sun, deep in the middle of the state's vast

landscapes. They pictured a world in which

high school students, full of promise but

limited by problems, would rise above their

situations and live healthy, eager lives. So,

the "Just Keep Livin" Foundation was

made. It is a lighthouse of hope that tells

young people to keep going and just keep living.

Many of these schools have an alarmingly high failure rate of 50%. The loud laughing in the cafeteria often covers the sad fact that 83% of the students line up with tickets for free or reduced meals. This is a sharp reminder of how much they have to deal with at such a young age. But it's not just about problems with money. Sad to say, children from poorer families are almost five times more likely to be abused or neglected than children from wealthier families.

With such scary numbers, Matthew and Camila McConaughey realized that their goal wasn't just to get people to exercise or eat better. It was about laying the groundwork for strength, desire, and health. The "J.K. Livin Foundation" stands tall as proof of how much they care. Not only is it a cause, but it is also a movement. A program that gives high school students the tools they need to follow their dreams and the belief that they deserve a future full of health, happiness, and endless opportunities.

CHAPTER FOUR

A CHRONOLOGY OF MCCONAUGHEY'S CONTROVERSIES

The Controversy Surrounding McConaughey's Vaccine Stance on Children

In the ever-changing world of 2021, Matthew McConaughey got a lot of attention, not for his movie parts, but for his opinion on a very important global issue: kid vaccine. In an honest interview with the New York Times, the star of "Interstellar" said that he and the other people in his family had been vaccinated against COVID-19, but he wasn't sure about vaccinating his younger children.

This statement got the reporters all worked up. As news stories and talk grew, McConaughey felt he had to explain what he meant. He took to Instagram to talk about how upset he was about being misquoted. His worry was only about the law that says kids 5–11 must get vaccinated. He didn't say he was against all child vaccinations. In fact, his 13-year-old son Levi had been given a shot to protect him from the virus.

Fans of McConaughey were confused by this kind of stance. A year ago, the star was a strong supporter of wearing masks. He even posted pictures of himself in nature while wearing a mask. Fans were confused by the difference between how he used to tell people to take safety steps and how he now feels about vaccinating children.

When he was asked about making vaccinations a school requirement, McConaughey's views were brought out even more in the New York Times interview. Even though he talked about how his family takes care of their health, he didn't want to make children get shots.

The US Surgeon General, Dr. Vivek Murthy, reacted quickly and emphasized how dangerous Covid-19 is for kids. When he talked on CNN, he added a personal touch by talking about when his own child was in the hospital because of another sickness. He stressed that no parent should have to go through that. With more and more children being hospitalized because of Covid, his worry was shared by many.

There were rumors that McConaughey might want to run for office, which added to the mystery. People talked a lot about him running for governor of Texas. Early polls showed that he was even ahead of Greg Abbot, who was already governor.

Given how controversial the discussion about vaccinations is in Texas, McConaughey's opinion could have a big impact on where he goes in politics. Some Texans believed strongly in the vaccine, but a large number still had doubts. Time would tell if this part of McConaughey's life would help or hurt his chances of running for office.

Naked Dance

Even big stars like Matthew McConaughey have their share of unexpected drama in the glitzy world of Hollywood. A very shocking thing that happened in 1999 is still written down in the history of famous

scandals. Imagine a Texas night, a house

with open windows bathed in soft

moonlight, and McConaughey enjoying his

own company. Lost in Henri Dikongué's

rhythmic African music, he decided to

dance naked while smoking a pipe and

letting the music wash over him.

But this peaceful scene didn't last for very

long. The Austin cops thought he was

doing some strange things, so they chose

to step in. When they broke into his

house, they found the star naked. They

put him in handcuffs and charged him

with a long list of crimes, including

fighting arrest, disturbing the peace, and

having pot. But McConaughey stood his

ground. He was angry and upset. He

shouted back and refused to get dressed.

This act of defiance was a statement to

him. He did not see his actions as being

morally or ethically incorrect; he was just

having a private moment in his own

house.

Later, he wrote about this interesting event

in his book "Greenlights." What came next?

A rather small fine of $50 and a lot of press

interest. But McConaughey came out on

top in a way, because the city of Austin

agreed with him. Soon, people were seen wearing 'BONGO NAKED' T-shirts, turning a scandal into a funny local tradition.

Involvement in Politics

Rumors about McConaughey's growing role in national conversations got stronger. Notably, these were places that were usually not related to his skill in movies or his promotion of Lincoln cars. McConaughey seemed to lean more into this new image as the public mood changed and it became possible for a famous Hollywood face to move up the political ladder. He gave the public hints that he might run for governor of Texas, and then he stepped forward to try to be a leader during tough times in Texas and even the whole country.

The way people saw it was, in fact, all over the place. Some people liked that he got involved in politics, but others were not as accepting. They were especially annoyed by how unclear McConaughey's statements often were. But in his book, he gave an idea of how he felt about politics by happily telling stories about how his family tree was full of rebels and unapologetic libertarians. This new

information made his political views
clearer and set the stage for how he would
react to the scary event at Robb
Elementary.

McConaughey's Heartfelt Response to a Hometown Tragedy

Matthew McConaughey's touching words
at the White House news meeting spread
through social media and touched people
all over the world. He stood at the stage
and told disturbing stories about the
terrible school tragedy that happened in
his city in 2021. His voice was shaking with
emotion. He painted a very clear picture of
Maite Rodriguez, a young girl whose green

Converse high-tops had a hand-drawn heart on them to show how much she loved the Earth. Even though it was a small thing, it was the only way for officials to find out who someone was in the chaos. He also talked about Alithia Ramirez, a ten-year-old girl who wanted to walk the streets of Paris, which were full of art.

There was a long, heavy silence in the room as McConaughey, who looked very upset, tried hard not to cry. His angry fist slammed into the podium, giving voice to the grief and anger that had gripped the whole country for the past two weeks.

Some doubters might say it was all an act, but anyone who looked closely could see that McConaughey's pain was real.

The Call for a Safer America

School, for him, seemed to have missed its mark entirely. McConaughey's deep sadness was clear, but at that moment, he made it clear that every American should look inward and figure out what they really need and what they just want. Still, the Matthew McConaughey of that week was changing and becoming more daring.

It all started when the actor wrote an opinion piece that was printed in the

Austin-American   Statesman.   Here,

McConaughey didn't just say the same

things we've heard before about the need

for unity. Instead, he laid out clear policy

changes and pushed for barriers that

would make it harder for people to use AR-

15s to do dangerous things. His rallying cry

was for universal background checks, the

creation of "red flag" laws, required waiting

times for buying assault guns, and raising

the age limit for buying such weapons from

18 to 21.

But McConaughey knew there were many

sides to the problem. The fall of American

ideals, the hunger for sensationalist media,

serious mental health issues, and the need for school safety were all important issues that needed to be addressed. Even though he recognized these bigger worries, he also stressed how urgent the problem of gun crime is. He knew that there would be counterarguments, so he pushed for quick, practical answers to stop the number of heartbreaking events from getting worse.

Even if McConaughey had just told the victims' stories in his White House speech, it would have had a deep impact. His fame made sure that their stories stayed in the news, and his skill at telling stories made sure that the whole country would remember, so that the pain wouldn't be

forgotten.

CHAPTER FIVE

CONCLUSION

McConaughey, from a young age, he embarked on his journey with unwavering determination, pursuing his dreams with great dedication. Today, his efforts have borne fruit, as he has achieved recognition as a celebrated actor and garnered a substantial following within the entertainment industry.

Matthew McConaughey's story is one of the most interesting and complex in the story of the 21st century, which is a long one with many twists and turns. Here is a man who is famous for his work in movies, but his real life is just as interesting as any part he's ever played. Hollywood's "golden boy" was once associated with the carefree charm of sun-kissed beaches and freewheeling parts, but he would eventually find himself at the center of important social arguments and controversies.

McConaughey's personal adventures, like his famous naked bongo dance, were big news in the calm nights of Texas. But as the years went by, so did the man's depth. McConaughey showed that he wasn't just an actor who was out of touch with reality by asking vaccine requirements for young children during a global pandemic and facing the sad truth of school deaths. Instead, he was a person who cared deeply about the most important issues of his time.

The Hollywood star was no longer just a face on a movie ad; he became a voice that spoke to millions of people. His speeches, whether they were in the New York Times or on the White House stage, showed a man who was struggling with his views and trying to blend his own experiences with a bigger story about society. His potential switch into a political figure, which was hinted at by reports and proved by his quick actions during emergencies, showed a big change.

But it wasn't just what he said that made people pay attention; it was actions that spoke louder. His well-thought-out policies, his focus on unity in a time of separation, and his earnest efforts to help people who had been hurt showed that he cared about where his country was going.

Still, in the middle of all these deep times, it's important to remember where

McConaughey came from. His personal stories, like the ones written about in "Greenlights," showed people the real, unvarnished person he was. He was just as real when he was thinking about things as when he was having fun.

By telling the story of McConaughey's life, we are asked to think about our own. Life doesn't go in a straight line or follow a plan. It is a series of scenes, and each one has its own highs and lows. There are funny parts and sad parts. Through McConaughey's life, we learn how important it is to enjoy every stage and to realize that the sum of all our experiences is what really makes our memory. In a world where news stories and trends come and go, McConaughey's life is a testament to the power of being real, being strong, and always believing in what you believe in.

Made in United States
Troutdale, OR
12/21/2024

27097385R00066